THE SCIENCE OF FUN

THE SCIENCE OF SNOW FUN

BY R. L. VAN

CONTENT CONSULTANT
Matthew R. Kumjian, PhD
Associate Professor of Meteorology
Pennsylvania State University

Core Library

An Imprint of Abdo Publishing
abdobooks.com

Cover image: Science explains how tubing down a snowy hill works.

abdobooks.com

Published by Abdo Publishing, a division of ABDO, PO Box 398166, Minneapolis, Minnesota 55439. Copyright © 2022 by Abdo Consulting Group, Inc. International copyrights reserved in all countries. No part of this book may be reproduced in any form without written permission from the publisher. Core Library™ is a trademark and logo of Abdo Publishing.

Printed in the United States of America, North Mankato, Minnesota
052021
092021

Cover Photo: Tammy Kay Photo/Shutterstock Images
Interior Photos: iStockphoto, 4–5, 7, 9, 22–23, 34–35, 37, 39; Shutterstock Images, 10, 14–15, 18, 25, 27, 43, 45; Alexey Kljatov/Shutterstock Images, 12; Vera Petrunina/iStockphoto, 17; Solveig Been/Shutterstock Images, 28; Katarzyna Wojtasik/Shutterstock Images, 30–31

Editor: Marie Pearson
Series Designer: Katharine Hale

Library of Congress Control Number: 2020948189

Publisher's Cataloging-in-Publication Data

Names: Van, R. L., author.
Title: The science of snow fun / by R. L. Van
Description: Minneapolis, Minnesota : Abdo Publishing, 2022 | Series: The science of fun | Includes online resources and index.
Identifiers: ISBN 9781532195198 (lib. bdg.) | ISBN 9781644946138 (pbk.) | ISBN 9781098215507 (ebook)
Subjects: LCSH: Snow--Juvenile literature. | Winter sports--Juvenile literature. | Force and energy--Juvenile literature. | Physics--Juvenile literature. | Dynamics--Juvenile literature. | Motion--Juvenile literature.
Classification: DDC 531.1--dc23

CONTENTS

SNOW DAY

Maya woke up to the smell of pancakes. But it was a Wednesday. Her dad only made pancakes on the weekends. She went downstairs to find her brother eating a blueberry pancake. He grinned and showed her his phone. Their school had sent out an alert. It was a snow day!

Maya looked out the window. There was a thick blanket of snow outside. Big, fluffy snowflakes were still falling. She scarfed

When it snows, many kids enjoy having fun outside.

down her pancakes. Then she messaged her neighborhood friends.

She met her friends in the backyard. Everyone wore their snow pants and winter boots. Maya gathered snow in a ball and rolled it around. Both of her friends did the same. Maya's snowball got bigger with each roll. The snow stuck together. Soon the ball was up to her knees.

Maya and her friends stacked the snowballs on top of each other. The biggest one was on the bottom. The smaller ones balanced on top of it. They found sticks for arms. Maya grabbed a carrot for its nose. Rocks made perfect eyes.

The snowman was finished. Then Maya's brother came outside. He threw a snowball at Maya's back and shouted, "Snowball fight!" Maya's snow day was off to a perfect start.

WHAT IS SNOW?

Many kids who live in places where it snows look forward to snow days. People may not think of snow

Kids can decorate snow people in many ways.

days as opportunities to learn. But there's a lot of science behind playing in the snow. Knowing some of that science can make snow even more fun.

Snow is a form of precipitation. Precipitation is water in different forms that falls from the sky.

Snow comes from water vapor, which is the gas form of water. The water vapor collects on tiny pieces of sand or dust in the atmosphere. It forms clouds. Cloud particles are either liquid drops or tiny ice crystals. The temperature in the atmosphere affects which form cloud particles take. If it's below 32 degrees Fahrenheit (0°C), snow can form. This process starts when more water vapor molecules attach to the cloud particles.

Water molecules in the form of ice stick together in the shape

SNOW DAYS AROUND THE UNITED STATES

Some states get more snow than others. Cold states, such as Minnesota and Massachusetts, get more snow than warm states, such as Florida and Texas. But school districts in warm states might cancel school for snow more often than those in cold states. That is because warm states may not be prepared for snow. They don't have snowplows or salt for icy roads. However, cold states can get dangerously cold. School districts may cancel school if it's too cold for kids to get to school safely.

Snow is frozen water that falls from the sky.

of a hexagon. This is a shape with six sides. A snowflake starts as a hexagonal ice crystal. More water vapor molecules connect to the crystal. They often attach to each of the six sides. The crystal grows. The six corners of the hexagon form the arms of the crystal. Each of the arms gets longer. Crystals run into each other in the clouds. They can stick together. As the crystals grow and stick together, they become snowflakes.

NO TWO ARE ALIKE

No two snowflakes are exactly the same. Snowflakes are made up of trillions of water molecules. The molecules

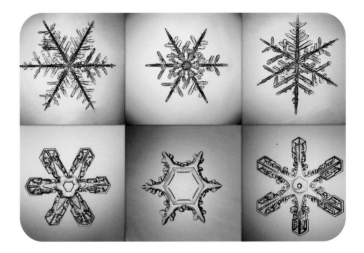

Every snowflake is unique.

can arrange themselves in many different ways within the hexagonal shape. There are so many possible combinations that identical snowflakes are very unlikely.

Many things affect the way snowflakes form. The temperature in the atmosphere is one factor. Crystals with long, skinny arms form when clouds have more moisture. Solid, platelike crystals form when clouds are drier. At certain moisture levels, side branches form on the arms.

As snowflakes grow, they become heavy. They begin to fall. The snowflake's shape changes as it falls. That is because the temperature and moisture in the air change. Each of the six branches on a snowflake forms the same way. The branches are identical to each other. This is because they have all been through the same conditions.

But branches on other flakes have been through slightly different conditions. They take different paths through the cloud. So they form a bit differently. This is why snowflakes are unique.

If it is cold enough on the ground, the snow builds up. Each individual snowflake changes, even on the ground.

SNOWFLAKE BENTLEY

Wilson "Snowflake" Bentley was born in 1865. He got a microscope when he was 15 years old. He wanted to take a picture of a snowflake. But snow melts quickly. Bentley set up his equipment outside so the snowflake wouldn't melt. He connected his microscope to a camera. Using a feather, he moved a snowflake under the microscope lens. In 1885, he took the first photograph of a snowflake. He took many more pictures of snowflakes. Each snowflake had a different pattern.

HOW SNOW FORMS

This graphic illustrates snow being formed in clouds. Compare this illustration to the description of snow formation in the text. Does the image help you better understand the text?

Snowflakes may melt and freeze again. Wind may break the snowflakes into smaller pieces. More snow may fall and press down on the snow beneath it.

People affect the snow on the ground too. Activities such as snow building, snowboarding, and snowmobiling move and pack the snow. There's a lot of science behind how these activities work.

STRAIGHT TO THE
SOURCE

Adam Watson is an ecologist, mountaineer, and environmentalist. He described his first memory of snow. He was seven years old and living in Turriff, Scotland:

> I could see these pale veils coming out of the sky, and as it got near the ground I saw they were actually snowflakes. . . . I picked up snow in my hand. . . . I was amazed by how fluffy and feathery it was. I could see the individual crystals, and how they varied— I didn't know then that they were all different, of course. But the other thing that struck me was just how quiet everything was. I lived in the [center] of this village and it was normally a noisy, busy place, but the snow deadened the sound. There was snow on every tree, every pavement, covering all the roads and so on. It had become a quiet world.

Source: Charlie English. "Doctor Watson's Feeling for Snow." *Guardian*, 6 Feb. 2009, theguardian.com. Accessed 5 May 2020.

WHAT'S THE BIG IDEA?

Read this passage carefully. What is the main point Watson is trying to make? Consider how that main idea is supported by details. Write down two or three supporting details that Watson uses to make his point.

SNOW CREATIONS

Once snow is on the ground, it's used for all sorts of activities. People have snowball fights and build snow people. Some types of snow are better for these activities than others. The weather plays a big role in the texture of each snowfall.

LET'S STICK TOGETHER

Not all snow is the same. Scientists put snow into five categories. They compare the amount of liquid water to the amount of ice crystals in

Sticky snow is great for making snowballs.

the snow. This determines whether snow is dry, moist, wet, very wet, or slush. Dry snow has no liquid water in it. Moist snow is less than 3 percent liquid. Wet snow is 3 percent to 8 percent liquid. Very wet snow is 8 percent to 15 percent liquid. Slush is more than 15 percent liquid.

Moist or wet snow sticks together best. The snow packs together. It's easy to shape and add to it. Dry snow doesn't have water to help keep the crystals together. The snow just crumbles. But wet snow and slush have too much water. All that liquid prevents the snow from holding a shape.

Air temperature is the main factor in making snow wet or dry. The colder it is, the greater the percentage of each snowflake will be frozen. Dry snow forms in colder air conditions than wet or moist snow.

SCIENCE AND SNOW PEOPLE

There are other things to consider when building a snow person besides the wetness of the snow. A snow

Snow that is too wet or dry won't stick together well.

person needs to be stable. The common round sections of a snow person are ideal for helping it stay upright. When making a section, people pack snow together into a sphere. Packing the snow together in a ball puts pressure on the ice crystals. This increases their temperature, causing the ice crystals to get stickier. The ice crystals stick together even better. But snow spheres can get too big. When the spheres are large, it is hard for a person to apply enough force when packing.

Packing snow in a ball helps snowflakes stick together.

Spheres are also ideal because they melt more slowly. They have less surface area compared to other shapes. This means less of the snow is exposed to the sun and heat.

Snow people are often built out of three balls of snow. There is one large ball at the base, one medium ball in the middle, and one small ball on top. Engineering helps explain why this is a popular design. Engineering is a form of science that in part studies how to make stable structures.

The bottom of the snow person needs to be big enough to support the top. Engineers have suggested ratios for building the perfect snow person. One ratio is 3:2:1. This means the diameter of the bottom

HUGE SNOW PERSON

People in Maine built a huge snow woman named Olympia in February 2008. She was more than 120 feet (37 m) tall. This is nearly as tall as the Statue of Liberty. Engineers and volunteers built a huge base of snow. Then snow was packed into flat disks. These disks of snow were stacked on the base in layers. The layers became smaller as they were stacked higher. Building Olympia took a lot of supplies. She required 13 million pounds (6 million kg) of snow. She had arms made from spruce trees. Her eyelashes were made from skis.

sphere of the snow person is three times the diameter of the top. Diameter is the width of a sphere. For example, the bottom sphere's diameter could be 3 feet (0.9 m). The middle sphere would have a diameter of 2 feet (0.6 m). The top sphere's diameter would be 1 foot (0.3 m). Getting out a tape measure isn't necessary for building a snow person. But it can help make the snow person sturdier.

MONKEYING AROUND

There are many animals that play in the snow. But one type of monkey called the Japanese macaque does something unique. These monkeys are also called snow monkeys. They make snowballs for fun. They roll them around in the snow to make even bigger snowballs. Then they carry their snowballs around. The monkeys even try to steal each other's snowballs!

SNOWBALL FIGHT!

As with building a snow person, packing snow is one important part of making snowballs. Packing the snowball tightly makes it dense. A dense snowball has more mass than a lightly packed snowball of the same size. Mass is the amount of matter in an object.

The density of a snowball affects how far it can be thrown. When a snowball flies through the air, it runs into air particles. This slows it down. Two snowballs of the same size will experience the same amount of resistance. But it takes less resistance to slow down a lighter object. The lighter snowball will slow down faster. The denser snowball will fly farther.

EXPLORE ONLINE

Chapter Two discusses the science behind why some snow sticks together. The article at the website below goes into more depth on this topic. How is the information from the website the same as the information in Chapter Two? What new information did you learn from the website?

WINNING THE SNOWBALL FIGHT: THE SCIENCE OF SNOW

abdocorelibrary.com/science-snow-fun

CHAPTER THREE

ALL DOWNHILL FROM HERE

Part of the excitement of winter is the chance to zoom down snowy hills. Some families go on ski trips. Kids may go to their neighborhood sledding hill. Skiing and snowboarding are major events at the Olympic Games. These activities give people the chance to race down the slopes. And physics plays a big role in all of these downhill snow sports.

Skiing is one of many popular sports involving snow.

THE SLEDDING HILL

There are many different forces at work in sledding. Isaac Newton's laws of motion help explain some of those forces. Newton was a scientist and mathematician. He lived from 1642 until 1727. Part of Newton's first law of motion says that something that isn't moving will stay still until a force moves it.

A boy might go sledding. He sits at the top of the hill in his sled. He can't go anywhere unless a force acts on him to move him down the hill. A few different things can move him. He can push himself. Another person can push him. Or, if he's already on a slope, gravity can pull him down. Gravity is a force that pulls objects toward Earth's center.

Newton's second law of motion says that acceleration happens when a force acts on a mass. It says that the amount of force acting on something affects how much the object speeds up or slows down. It also explains that items with more mass need more

A push from a friend can provide the force needed to put a sled in motion.

force to accelerate. So the boy in the sled will move differently depending on his weight and on the strength of the forces that push him.

The boy's little brother might push him. His little brother can't push with much force. The boy will accelerate a little. But if a stronger adult pushes him, he will accelerate more. The adult can apply more force.

STOP AND GO

Once enough force acts on the boy, he accelerates. He is in motion. As he slides down the hill, he speeds up. Gravity pulls on him. It makes him go faster. He can go faster on a steep hill than on a flatter hill. This is because gravity acts straight down toward Earth's center. On a gentle slope, much of the force of gravity is pushing down on the ground. Gravity will not give the sled much speed. On a steeper slope, more of the gravity is speeding up the sled.

Newton's first law of motion also says that an object in motion will keep moving until a force stops it or changes its motion. The boy in the sled has a few things slowing him down as he rides down the hill. Gravity pulls down on him less when he reaches the bottom of the hill. This is because he's no longer on a slope. He can't go any farther down. Friction also slows him down.

A steep hill with packed snow can make sleds go very fast.

Friction is when two things rub against each other. This rubbing resists motion.

People want low friction when they go sledding. Packed snow provides a smooth surface. The smooth plastic of a sled sliding over packed snow doesn't cause as much friction as sliding over fluffy, loose snow. But even on packed snow, there is some friction. The friction creates heat. It melts some of the snow.

SLEDDING FORCES

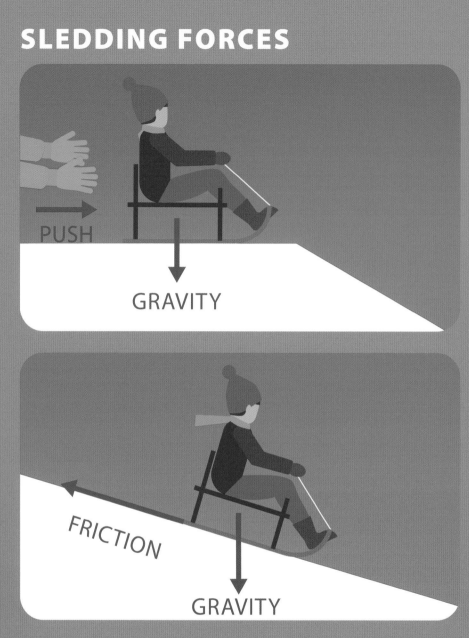

PUSH

GRAVITY

FRICTION

GRAVITY

These illustrations show the different forces that act on someone sledding. Does seeing these illustrations help you understand the text better? Can you think of any other forces that might be acting on this sledder that aren't shown in the images?

This forms a layer of water. The water reduces friction. The sled glides more easily. But at the bottom of the hill, gravity is no longer keeping the sled in motion. Friction eventually stops the sled.

DOWNHILL SKILL

Just like sledders, skiers and snowboarders have to deal with friction. Athletes do a lot of different things to reduce friction. Skiers wax the bottoms of

MAKING SNOW

Many ski hills and resorts have snow machines. They use these to make their own snow when there isn't enough natural snow on the ground. Snow machines send tiny pieces of ice high into the air. Then they spray drops of water at those particles. The drops of water freeze onto the pieces of ice. The ice and water become frozen grains of snow. These grains of snow don't have branches like natural snowflakes. They are dense, rounded balls. This shape makes the snow harder. It also helps it last longer. The denser human-made snow doesn't melt as quickly as natural snow.

Snowboarders use gravity to help them do tricks on a half-pipe.

their skis. This reduces friction between the skis and the snow. Just like in sledding, the friction between a ski and the snow heats up and melts a layer of snow. With wax, the melted snow beads up on the ski. The water touches less area on each ski. This means there is even less friction between the water and the ski. Snowboarders wax the bottoms of their snowboards for the same reason.

For some snowboarders, an important part of their sport is doing tricks. Snowboarders doing tricks work with the force of gravity differently than if they were racing downhill. Some tricks are performed on a half-pipe. This is a downhill ramp shaped like a U. Snowboarders use the pull of gravity to build speed while going downhill as they enter the half-pipe.

SCIENCE OF SPEED

Skiing is faster than snowboarding. That is because it is easier for people to keep their weight balanced between the two skis. Snowboarders have to move their bodies around more to keep their balance on the board. Also, skiers can tuck themselves in to reduce wind resistance. When snowboarders tuck, they have more surface area exposed to the air. The fastest speed a skier has reached is 158 miles per hour (254 km/h). The fastest speed a snowboarder has reached is 126 miles per hour (203 km/h). That's still fast. But skiing wins the race!

Snowboarders can jump as they enter the half-pipe. This gives them a greater distance to fall into it. There is more time for gravity to help them accelerate. Speed helps snowboarders go up the other side of the half-pipe. With enough speed, they can soar above the half-pipe. Eventually, gravity will pull them back down again. They slide back down the U shape. They gain speed to launch themselves up the other side again.

STRAIGHT TO THE
SOURCE

Jessie Diggins is an Olympic cross-country skier and gold medalist. She's also a climate change activist. She talks about the ways that climate change is affecting snow:

> Over the last 10 years, it has been hard to ski on real snow. Over the last three years, most venues have been exclusively on man-made snow. And in places like Davos, Switzerland, where they normally have three feet [1 m] of snow, they've been snow farming and saving it for the next year because they don't even count on getting snow anymore. . . .

> [Skiing on human-made snow is] a little faster. So the same World Cup courses that we race get more and more dangerous with man-made snow because it gets icy.

> Source: Henry Fountain, et al. "This Olympic Skier Wants to Save the World's Snow." *New York Times*, 7 Feb. 2018, nytimes.com. Accessed 6 May 2020.

BACK IT UP

In this passage, Diggins is using evidence to support her point. Write a paragraph describing the point Diggins is making. Then write down two or three pieces of evidence she uses to make this point.

SNOW TREK

Some snow activities take place across long distances. Hiking on dirt trails in warmer months is easy. But it can take special equipment to explore the outdoors when snow covers the ground.

SNOWSHOES AND SKIS

One of the challenges of walking in deep snow is staying on top of it. People's feet often sink into deep snow. Snowshoes or cross-country skis help keep people on top of the snow.

Snowshoeing can be a fun way to enjoy the outdoors.

This is because of pressure. The force of a person's weight pushes onto the snow. Without snowshoes, all of a person's weight is balanced on his or her feet. This puts a large amount of pressure on small areas of the snow. With snowshoes, the weight is spread across a greater surface area. A person can walk on top of the snow without sinking in.

Cross-country skis are similar to snowshoes in some ways. They have greater surface area than feet. They spread a person's weight out over more area. This helps cross-country skiers stay above

SNOWSHOE PAWS

Lynx, snowshoe hares, and some other critters living in snowy places have a special trait that helps them survive snowy conditions. This trait is large paws. Large paws act like snowshoes. They spread out weight. Snowshoe hares and lynx can also spread out the toes on their large paws. This creates even more surface area. A bird called the ptarmigan has feather-covered feet. The feathers increase the surface area of its feet. The ptarmigan can walk on top of the snow.

Cross-country skiers use friction to help them move.

the snow. But skis are much longer than snowshoes. They have more contact area with the ground in the front and in back of a skier. It is harder to fall forward or backward. But they don't give much balance to the sides.

Cross-country skis are similar to downhill skis. They are waxed on the bottoms. But cross-country skiers use wax in a different way. A cross-country skier wants to move forward. To do that, she needs to slide one ski forward. The wax will help that ski glide just like it does for downhill skis. But the ski on her other foot needs to stay put. She presses down with her foot. This lets the wax on this ski develop traction with the snow. It lets the skier push off with the stable leg and add more force into her moving leg.

Cross-country skis have areas on the bottom called grip zones. They help increase traction. Grip zones often have bumps that angle toward the back of the ski, similar to a fish's scales. When a skier pulls the ski backward against the snow, the scalelike bumps push against the snow. This stops the ski from moving backward. When the skier moves that ski forward, the pieces slide over the snow. They don't create much friction.

SNOW SPEED

Snowmobiles are the fastest way to speed through the snow. Most can reach top speeds of 95 to 120 miles per hour (155–195 km/h). They have a lot of different features to make snow travel easier. Snowmobiles have

People in snowy areas sometimes travel by snowmobile.

skis on the front. Riders turn them to steer. The machines also have tracks in the back. The tracks push the snowmobile forward. The tracks are like tires. But they are shaped differently. They are longer. They are flat where they come in contact with the ground. Longer tracks work the same way snowshoes do. They have contact with the snow over a wide area. This spreads

SNOWMOBILE ON WATER

Snowmobiles aren't only for snow! Some people compete in snowmobile watercross. They drive modified snowmobiles over water. The snowmobiles can weigh up to 400 pounds (180 kg). They need to go approximately 15 miles per hour (24 km/h) to stay on top of the water. They stay on top of the water because of opposing forces. The snowmobile pushes the water down. The water pushes the snowmobile up. The treads push the snowmobile forward. They act like propellers. The snowmobile is tipped up slightly as it moves. This helps to keep the water from pushing over the top of the snowmobile.

out the weight of the snowmobile so it doesn't sink into the snow.

Snowmobile tracks also help with traction. Tracks have a large surface area and rough treads. Some snowmobilers add sharp pieces to their tracks. All of these features help the tracks create friction with slippery surfaces. They have better grip than regular tires.

Science plays a role in any kind

of snow activity. Building a snow person, sledding downhill, and taking a hike in snowshoes can all be better understood with science. Science can help people get better at these activities. It can help skiers go faster, snowboarders fly higher, and snowball fighters throw farther. Science makes snow even more fun!

FURTHER EVIDENCE

Chapter Four describes many different methods of traveling and exploring in snow. What is one of the main points of the chapter? What evidence is used to support this point? Read the article at the website below. Does the information in the article support the main point you identified? Does it present new evidence?

LET'S GO SNOWSHOEING!

abdocorelibrary.com/science-snow-fun

FAST FACTS

- Snowflakes, also called ice crystals, form when water vapor sticks together.

- Snowflakes can arrange themselves in many different ways, and they form differently depending on the conditions they go through. This is why no two snowflakes are identical.

- Moist and wet snow sticks together best because of the amount of liquid in the snow.

- A knowledge of engineering can help when building snow people. People can make the structures stable so they won't fall over easily.

- Downhill snow sports, such as sledding, skiing, and snowboarding, demonstrate Newton's laws of motion. Objects stay still unless a force moves them. They continue moving unless a force slows them down. More force is required to move or stop objects with more mass.

- Friction from sleds, skis, or snowboards rubbing against the snow creates a thin layer of water. The water has less friction with these items than snow does, so people riding them go faster.

- Snowshoes distribute a person's weight across a greater surface area than feet. This means that there is less pressure in each square inch of the snowshoe pushing down on the snow. Other objects, including cross-country skis, do the same thing. This keeps people from sinking into deep snow.

- Moving across snow requires traction in order to generate the force needed to move forward. Bumps on cross-country skis give the skis traction on snowy surfaces.

STOP AND THINK

Surprise Me

Chapter Two discusses the science of building snow people. After reading this book, what two or three facts about building snow people did you find most surprising? Write a few sentences about each fact. Why did you find each fact surprising?

Dig Deeper

After reading this book, what questions do you still have about the science of skiing and snowboarding? With an adult's help, find a few reliable sources that can help you answer your questions. Write a paragraph about what you learned.

Say What?

Studying the science of snow and winter activities can mean learning a lot of new vocabulary. Find five words in this book you've never heard before. Use a dictionary to find out what they mean. Then write the meanings in your own words and use each word in a new sentence.

You Are There

Chapter Three describes the science of snowboarding in a half-pipe. Imagine you are at the Winter Olympics watching this event. Write a letter home telling your friends what you saw. What do you notice about different athletes' performances? Be sure to add plenty of detail to your note.

GLOSSARY

acceleration
a change in an
object's speed

atmosphere
the layers of gases around
Earth, including the air living
things breathe

force
something that pushes or
pulls on an object, affecting
the way it moves

molecule
a group of atoms, which
are the smallest units of an
element, that make up the
smallest unit of a compound,
such as water

pressure
the amount of force pressing
on a certain area

ratio
a relationship in amount or
size between two or more
things, shown with numbers

surface area
the amount of space
that the surfaces of a
three-dimensional object
take up

traction
the friction between
two objects that makes
them stick together and
increases grip

tread
the pattern of bumps and
grooves on an object that
helps it develop traction with
a surface

ONLINE RESOURCES

To learn more about the science of snow fun, visit our free resource websites below.

Visit **abdocorelibrary.com** or scan this QR code for free Common Core resources for teachers and students, including vetted activities, multimedia, and booklinks, for deeper subject comprehension.

Visit **abdobooklinks.com** or scan this QR code for free additional online weblinks for further learning. These links are routinely monitored and updated to provide the most current information available.

LEARN MORE

London, Martha. *The Science of Water Parks*. Abdo Publishing, 2021.

McKinney, Donna B. *STEM in Snowboarding*. Abdo Publishing, 2018.

INDEX

About the Author

R. L. Van is a writer and editor living in the Twin Cities, Minnesota. She has written nonfiction books on a variety of subjects. In her free time, she enjoys reading, doing crossword puzzles, and caring for her pet cats.